All About Mom and Me

all about MOM and ME

A Journal for Mothers and Daughters

Janene Dutt

Illustrated by Alyssa Gonzalez

ROCKRIDGE
PRESS

For general information on our other products and services or to obtain technical support, please contact our Customer Care Department within the United States at (866) 744-2665, or outside the United States at (510) 253-0500.

Rockridge Press publishes its books in a variety of electronic and print formats. Some content that appears in print may not be available in electronic books, and vice versa.

Interior and Cover Designer: Lindsey Dekker
Art Producer: Samantha Ulban
Editor: Brian Sweeting
Production Editor: Emily Sheehan
Photography/Illustrations © Alyssa Gonzalez, 2020

ISBN: Print 978-1-64876-604-6
R0

This journal belongs to:

_____

A Note to Moms

If there is one sound every mother of a daughter will eventually hear, it's the sound of a slammed door. I remember doing some frequent door slamming myself as a ten-year-old. I was an introverted child who preferred books to conversations, and my yellow Snoopy-covered diary was my trusty confidante. I would vent about my annoying little brother, a bad grade on a test, and, of course, my mother. Then I would carefully hide my diary under my mattress, lest my true feelings ever be revealed.

Fast-forward to my life 30 years later: I now have two daughters of my own. Raising girls is not for the faint of heart. It is rewarding, challenging, humbling, and oftentimes an emotional roller-coaster ride for both mother and daughter.

I'll never forget the time my youngest, then nine years old, came home from school visibly upset. Despite my prying, she refused to tell me what was wrong. The more I questioned her, the more upset she got, until finally, she ran upstairs and—you guessed it—slammed her door.

Unsure of what to do, I decided to give her some space. A few minutes later, I was walking past her room when I saw a note slide under her door. It simply said, "I'm sad." My first reaction was to walk into her room to talk, but something in my gut told me not to. Instead, I grabbed the note, wrote back, and slid it back under her door.

The conversation continued this way, with each of us sitting on either side of the door. She began to open up about feeling ignored and excluded by her friends. And though she was too shy or embarrassed to say the words to my face, writing them down somehow made everything much more bearable.

And thus began our own little method of communication over the next few years. I knew that when she was overwhelmed, or sad, or angry, eventually a note would come sliding under the door—a note that, more often than not, would lead to a conversation that we may not have had otherwise.

And that brings us to this journal. If you're reading this, you've already taken the first step in strengthening the bond between you and your daughter. My hope is that, through the words that will be written here, you and your daughter will find honesty, humor, understanding, and support—and when the last entry is filled in, you'll have a beautiful keepsake to be treasured for years to come.

Enjoy!

—Janene

A Note to Daughters

My mom and I have been writing notes back and forth for a few years now. Sometimes it's hard for me to talk about things like friendship problems, and writing my feelings down helps. I think this journal is really useful if you are shy or too embarrassed to talk about something in person.

Also, I like learning more about what my mom's life was like when she was my age and reading the story of her most embarrassing moment, which was SUPER embarrassing!

I think the drawing section is cool too because I never really got to see my mom draw things before.

Writing with my mom makes me feel like she is really listening to me. I like that this journal is just for the two of us and nobody else. It's kind of like we have a little secret.

I hope you enjoy filling out this journal with your mom. I think that sharing your feelings and sharing stories with your mom will make you feel closer than you did before.

Have fun!

—Ava Dutt, age 12

Getting on the Same Page

From sharing embarrassing moments to describing your perfect day, this journal is an opportunity for the two of you to learn more about each other in a fun and creative way. Maybe you'll find out that your mom also hated broccoli as a kid. Perhaps your child's favorite memory is not what you would have guessed.

Before you begin writing, I encourage you to sit down and talk about how, exactly, this process will work. To make it easier, I'll share some guidelines that you can discuss together. If you just can't wait to start writing, it's okay to skip all that and jump right in! The "right" way to use this journal is whatever works best for the two of you.

Is This a Secret?

Something you may want to talk about is who else, if anyone, will be allowed to see this journal. If you decide it's just for the two of you, then you may need to brainstorm a great hiding spot to keep it safe from nosy family members!

Speaking of nosy family members, will you allow each other to talk about the journal with anyone else? Or will you pinky-swear that it'll be a mother-daughter secret forever? I think it's important that you both agree on this particular point—otherwise, there may be trouble if Aunt Edna mentions it over Thanksgiving dinner.

Filling Out Entries

What about filling out the entries themselves? Perhaps one of you is systematic and organized and would naturally fill out the journal in order, and the other is more spontaneous and creative and would like to write about whatever topic seems appealing at the moment. Does one of you choose the prompt on odd days and the other on even days? Discuss the best way to handle this so that you are both (literally!) on the same page.

Passing the Journal Back and Forth

You may also want to discuss how the journal will be passed back and forth. If the journal is being kept top secret, do you have different nightly drop locations and code names, like your own mother-daughter spy movie? Or will you simply leave it on each other's nightstands when you are done? Find a way that makes the most sense for both of you.

Setting a Schedule

Finally, talk about timing. Will you write in the journal every day? Once a week? And once the journal is passed to the other person, will there be a certain amount of time before you have to return it? Or maybe it will be totally flexible. Some days will be busier than others, and some days you just may not feel like writing at all. That's okay. Think of the journal as a marathon, not a sprint. This is a keepsake you'll have for many years, so taking care and time with it will only make it more valuable.

Keep in Mind

Now that you've set some guidelines for how to use the journal, here are some ideas to keep in mind when writing your entries.

Be Honest

Remember, this journal is a safe space in which to share your feelings. Maybe there's something you've been wanting to talk about but have been afraid to. The purpose of this experience is to develop a deeper understanding of each other, and being honest with your words and feelings is the best way to do that. Keeping an open mind when using this journal will ensure that both of you feel respected.

Listen to Each Other

There is an opportunity here to really listen to each other. With our busy schedules, we aren't always able to give people our full attention at the exact moment they want it. I know that sometimes my daughter is talking to me when I'm in the middle of making dinner or emailing someone, and it seems like I'm only half-listening. Cue the mom guilt! But she knows that when she hands me something she wrote, I will pretty much drop everything and read it. And when I write back, she will do the same. If there's one thing all moms and daughters have in common, it's that they both want to feel heard.

Have Fun

Above all else, this journal should be a fun activity for the two of you to share. Don't be afraid to be silly, creative, or think outside the box. In the drawing section, my daughter quickly found out that my artistic ability peaked at around fourth grade. Frankly, I think she was a little proud that her drawings were far better than mine! Sharing this space should never feel like a "have-to"—if there are times when one of you is just not feeling it, then step away for a while. I promise, the journal won't be offended, and it will still be there when you are inspired to write again.

Tell Stories

My daughter loves to hear the story of the day she was born. She loves to hear that I used to fight with my little brother. And she laughed hysterically when I told her about the time I accidentally walked around a mall with toilet paper hanging out of my pants. Every family has their stories . . . some are funny, some are sad, some are embarrassing. Sharing stories provides entertainment, unites us as a family, and gives us a deeper understanding of our past. The prompts in this journal will make it easy to transfer those stories from your memory to the page, where they can be relived over and over for many years to come.

Mother

Describe three things you admire about your daughter.

1 _____

_____

_____

2 _____

_____

_____

3 _____

_____

_____

 Daughter

Describe three things you admire about your mom.

1

_____

_____

_____

2

_____

_____

_____

3

_____

_____

_____

Mother

What is your favorite season?

_____

What are four things you like about this time of year?

1 _____

_____

2 _____

_____

3 _____

_____

4 _____

_____

Daughter

What is your favorite season?

_____

What are four things you like about this time of year?

1 _____

2 _____

3 _____

4 _____

Mother

Did you have a favorite pet as a child?

_____

_____

_____

_____

Do you have any stories about this pet?

_____

_____

_____

_____

Daughter

Do you have any pets? If yes, do you want any other pets? If no, do you want a pet?

_____

_____

_____

_____

_____

What is your favorite thing about your pet?

_____

_____

_____

_____

_____

_____

Mother

What's the nicest thing a friend has ever done for you?

_____

_____

_____

_____

What's the nicest thing you've ever done for a friend?

_____

_____

_____

_____

Daughter

What's the nicest thing a friend has ever done for you?

_____

_____

_____

_____

What's the nicest thing you've ever done for a friend?

_____

_____

_____

_____

_____

✧ Mother ✧

What would you do if you could trade places with your daughter for a day?

_____

_____

_____

_____

_____

_____

_____

_____

_____

_____

Daughter

What would you do if you could trade places with your mom for a day?

_____

_____

_____

_____

_____

_____

_____

_____

_____

_____

Mother

If you could rule the world for a day, what exactly would you do?

_____

_____

_____

_____

_____

_____

_____

_____

_____

_____

Daughter

If you could rule the world for a day, what exactly would you do?

_____

_____

_____

_____

_____

_____

_____

_____

_____

_____

Mother

In what ways are you most similar to your daughter?

_____

_____

_____

_____

_____

In what ways are you most different?

_____

_____

_____

_____

_____

Daughter

How are you and your mom alike?

_____

_____

_____

_____

_____

How are you and your mom different?

_____

_____

_____

_____

_____

Mother

What was your very first job? How much did you get paid?

_____

_____

_____

_____

What did you learn from this job?

_____

_____

_____

_____

_____

Daughter

If you could get a job right now, what would you want to do?

_____

_____

_____

_____

What would you do with the money you made?

_____

_____

_____

_____

_____

 Mother

Who is the person you find it easiest to talk to? Why did you choose this person?

_____

_____

_____

_____

Who do you trust the most?

_____

_____

_____

_____

 Daughter

Who is the person you find it easiest to talk to? Why did you choose this person?

_____

_____

_____

Who do you trust the most?

_____

_____

_____

Who is the person you would trust the most with a secret?

_____

_____

_____

 Mother

What is the best gift you've ever received?

_____

_____

_____

_____

What is the best gift you've ever given someone?

_____

_____

_____

_____

_____

✦ Daughter ✦

What is the best gift you've ever received?

_____

_____

_____

_____

What is the best gift you've ever given someone?

_____

_____

_____

_____

_____

Mother

Describe your daughter in five words.

1 _____
2 _____
3 _____
4 _____
5 _____

Describe yourself in five words.

1 _____
2 _____
3 _____
4 _____
5 _____

Daughter

Describe your mom in five words.

1 _____

2 _____

3 _____

4 _____

5 _____

Describe yourself in five words.

1 _____

2 _____

3 _____

4 _____

5 _____

Mother

Who is your favorite TV family?

_____

_____

_____

_____

_____

What are the qualities you admire about them?

_____

_____

_____

_____

_____

Daughter

Who is your favorite TV family?

_____

_____

_____

_____

Do you think it would be fun to be a part of this family? If yes, how?

_____

_____

_____

_____

_____

 Mother

Who was your favorite teacher as a child? Why?

_____

_____

_____

What was your favorite subject in school?

_____

_____

_____

What was your least favorite subject in school?

_____

_____

_____

Daughter

Who is your favorite teacher?

_____

_____

What is the best thing about this teacher?

_____

_____

What is your favorite subject in school?

_____

_____

What is your least favorite subject in school?

_____

_____

Mother

Things that make you laugh:

_____

_____

Things that make you cry:

_____

_____

Things that make you proud:

_____

_____

Things that make you excited:

_____

_____

Daughter

Things that make you laugh:

_____

_____

Things that make you cry:

_____

_____

Things that make you proud:

_____

_____

Things that make you excited:

_____

_____

Mother

What was your favorite vacation as a child?

_____

_____

_____

_____

Who did you go with, and what did you do there?

_____

_____

_____

_____

_____

Daughter

What is the best vacation you've been on?

_____

_____

_____

If you could pick any vacation spot, what would it be?

_____

_____

_____

Who would you bring on vacation with you?

_____

_____

_____

Mother

What is the best thing about your family?

_____

_____

_____

_____

_____

What is the most unusual thing about your family?

_____

_____

_____

_____

_____

_____

Daughter

What is the best thing about your family?

_____

_____

_____

_____

What is the most unusual thing about your family?

_____

_____

_____

_____

✦ Mother ✦

Draw a portrait of your daughter:

Daughter

Draw a portrait of your mom:

Mother

Tell a story about a time you got in trouble.

_____

_____

_____

_____

_____

What did you learn from that experience?

_____

_____

_____

_____

_____

Daughter

Tell a story about a time you got in trouble.

_____

_____

_____

_____

What did you learn from that experience?

_____

_____

_____

_____

Mother

What is your favorite holiday?

_____

What are three reasons why this holiday is your favorite?

1 _____

2 _____

3 _____

What is your favorite memory of this holiday?

_____

_____

_____

_____

_____

Daughter

What is your favorite holiday?

_____

What are three reasons why this holiday is your favorite?

1 _____

2 _____

3 _____

What is your favorite memory of this holiday?

_____

_____

_____

_____

Mother

What was your most embarrassing moment as a child?

_____

_____

_____

_____

_____

When were you most proud of yourself as a child?

_____

_____

_____

_____

_____

Daughter

What was your most embarrassing moment?

_____

_____

_____

_____

What was your proudest moment?

_____

_____

_____

_____

_____

 Mother

If you could have any superpower, what would it be?

_____

_____

_____

How would you use it to make the world a better place?

_____

_____

_____

_____

_____

_____

_____

Daughter

If you could have any superpower, what would it be?

_____

_____

_____

How would you use it to make the world a better place?

_____

_____

_____

_____

_____

_____

_____

Mother

How did you spend your summer days as a child?

_____

_____

_____

_____

_____

What things did you do that your daughter has not yet experienced?

_____

_____

_____

_____

_____

_____

Daughter

What's your favorite thing about summer?

_____

_____

_____

_____

What's one way your summer could be better?

_____

_____

_____

_____

Mother

What is your favorite breakfast?

_____

What is your favorite kind of cookie?

_____

What is one food you never get tired of?

_____

What is the most unusual food you've ever eaten?

_____

What is one food you never want to eat again?

_____

Daughter

What is your favorite breakfast?

_____

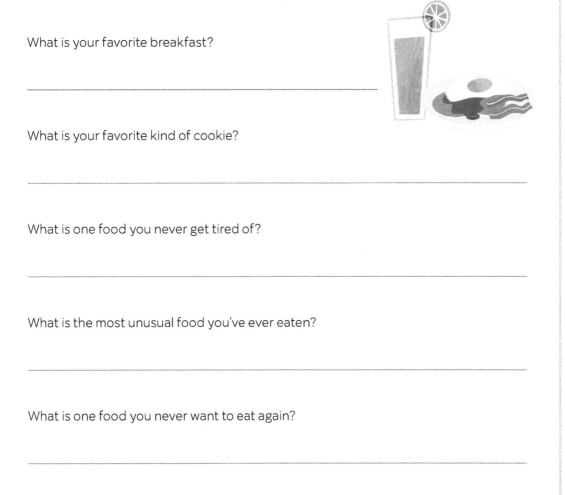

What is your favorite kind of cookie?

_____

What is one food you never get tired of?

_____

What is the most unusual food you've ever eaten?

_____

What is one food you never want to eat again?

_____

✧ Mother ✧

Describe a perfect day with your daughter.

_____

_____

_____

_____

✧ Daughter ✧

If you could plan a perfect day with your mom, where would you go and what would you do?

_____

_____

_____

_____

Mother

What is your favorite birthday memory?

_____

_____

_____

What is the worst birthday gift you've ever received?

_____

_____

_____

Have you ever had a surprise party?

_____

_____

_____

Daughter

What is your favorite birthday memory?

_____

_____

_____

What is the worst birthday gift you've ever received?

_____

_____

_____

Would you ever want a surprise party?

_____

_____

_____

What is an outdoor activity you'd like to do with your daughter?

_____

_____

Make plans to do it together! Afterward, share your thoughts on how it went. What did you enjoy about it?

_____

_____

_____

_____

_____

_____

_____

_____

Daughter

What is an outdoor activity you'd like to do with your mom?

_____

_____

Make plans to do it together! Afterward, share your thoughts on how it went. What did you enjoy about it?

_____

_____

_____

_____

_____

_____

_____

Mother

What is the best advice your parents ever gave you?

_____

_____

_____

_____

If you could make your daughter follow one piece of advice, what would it be?

_____

_____

_____

_____

_____

Daughter

What is the best advice your mom ever gave you?

_____

_____

_____

_____

If you could give your mom one piece of advice, what would it be?

_____

_____

_____

_____

_____

_____

Mother

Who is a leader who inspires you?

_____

_____

_____

_____

_____

What are the qualities that a leader should have?

_____

_____

_____

_____

_____

_____

 Daughter

Who is a leader who inspires you?

_____

_____

_____

_____

Would you want to be a leader? Why or why not?

_____

_____

_____

_____

Mother

You won the lottery! Draw how you would spend your money:

✦ Daughter ✦

You won the lottery! Draw how you would spend your money:

Mother

What did you eat for breakfast as a child?

_____

_____

_____

Did you bring lunch to school or did you buy lunch in the cafeteria?

_____

_____

_____

What was the best thing your parents made for dinner?

_____

_____

_____

Daughter

What foods do you usually eat for breakfast?

_____

_____

_____

Would you rather bring or buy your lunch?

_____

_____

_____

What's your favorite thing your mom makes for dinner?

_____

_____

_____

Mother

What is the best place you've ever been?

_____

What are three reasons that this place is special?

1 _____

_____

_____

2 _____

_____

_____

3 _____

_____

_____

 Daughter

What is the best place you've ever been?

_____

What are three reasons that this place is special?

1 _____

_____

_____

2 _____

_____

_____

3 _____

_____

_____

 Mother

When do you feel the strongest?

_____

_____

_____

_____

_____

When do you feel the weakest?

_____

_____

_____

_____

Daughter

When do you feel the strongest?

_____

_____

_____

_____

_____

When do you feel the weakest?

_____

_____

_____

_____

_____

Mother

Did you fight with your siblings or other family members growing up? If so, what did you fight about?

_____

_____

_____

_____

Did you like being the only/oldest/middle/youngest child? Why?

_____

_____

_____

_____

Daughter

Do you fight with your siblings or other family members? If so, what do you fight about the most?

_____

_____

_____

_____

Do you like being the only/oldest/middle/youngest child? Why?

_____

_____

_____

_____

Mother

What is your greatest talent?

_____

What are some talents you wish you had?

_____

Daughter

What is your greatest talent?

_____

What are some talents you wish you had?

_____

Mother

Did you have a favorite grandparent?

_____

_____

_____

What is something they taught you?

_____

_____

_____

What is your favorite memory involving them?

_____

_____

_____

Daughter

What is the best thing about your grandparents?

_____

_____

_____

What is one thing your grandparents have taught you?

_____

_____

_____

What is your favorite memory involving your grandparents?

_____

_____

_____

✦ Mother ✦

What is something your daughter does that makes you laugh?

_____

What's the funniest thing your daughter has ever said?

_____

✦ Daughter ✦

What is something your mom does that makes you laugh?

_____

What happened that made your mom laugh the most?

_____

 Mother

If you could invent one thing, what would it be?

_____

_____

_____

Why do you think this invention is needed?

_____

_____

_____

_____

_____

_____

_____

_____

Daughter

If you could invent one thing, what would it be?

_____

_____

_____

Why do you think this invention is needed?

_____

_____

_____

_____

_____

_____

 Mother

What was the hardest age for you growing up?

_____

What do you think would have made this age a little easier for you?

_____

_____

_____

_____

_____

_____

_____

_____

Daughter

If you could be any age, what age would you be?

_____

What do you think would be fun about being this age?

_____

_____

_____

_____

_____

_____

_____

_____

✦ Mother ✦

Have you ever lost a friendship?

_____

_____

Do you regret losing that friendship? Is there something you could have done to fix the friendship?

_____

_____

_____

_____

_____

_____

_____

Daughter

Have you ever had a fight with a friend?

_____

_____

How would you handle the situation differently next time?

_____

_____

_____

_____

_____

_____

_____

_____

✦ Mother ✦

What are three important things your daughter has taught you?

1 _____

2 _____

3 _____

✦ Daughter ✦

What are three important things your mom has taught you?

1 _____

2 _____

3 _____

Mother

Who is the bravest person you know?

_____

What makes them brave?

_____

_____

_____

_____

_____

_____

_____

_____

_____

Daughter

Who is the bravest person you know?

_____

What makes them brave?

_____

_____

_____

_____

_____

_____

_____

_____

 Mother

The best part of being a mom is:

_____

_____

_____

_____

_____

The hardest part of being a mom is:

_____

_____

_____

_____

_____

Daughter

The best part of being a kid is:

_____

_____

_____

_____

_____

The hardest part of being a kid is:

_____

_____

_____

_____

Mother

What was your favorite book as a child?

_____

What was your daughter's favorite book when she was little?

_____

Daughter

What is your favorite book?

_____

If you wrote a book, what would the title be?

_____

 Mother

What famous person would you most like to meet?

_____

How would you spend a day with them?

_____

_____

_____

_____

_____

_____

_____

_____

_____

Daughter

What famous person would you most like to meet?

_____

How would you spend a day with them?

_____

_____

_____

_____

_____

_____

_____

_____

Mother

Draw your dream house:

Daughter

Draw your dream house:

Mother

What language would you like to learn?

_____

How would speaking this language benefit you?

_____

_____

_____

_____

_____

_____

_____

_____

 Daughter

What language would you like to learn?

_____

How would speaking this language be helpful to you?

_____

_____

_____

_____

_____

_____

_____

_____

✧ Mother ✧

If you were granted three wishes, what would you wish for?

1 _____

2 _____

3 _____

✧ Daughter ✧

If you were granted three wishes, what would you wish for?

1 _____

2 _____

3 _____

Mother

What's the biggest difference between your childhood and your daughter's childhood?

_____

_____

_____

_____

What are some things that are the same?

_____

_____

_____

_____

_____

_____

Daughter

What do you think your mom's childhood was like?

_____

_____

_____

_____

Do you think it was harder or easier than yours? Why?

_____

_____

_____

_____

_____

_____

_____

 Mother

What keeps you up at night worrying?

_____

_____

_____

_____

Why do you think this scares you?

_____

_____

_____

_____

_____

Daughter

What is something that worries you?

_____

_____

_____

_____

_____

You would worry less about it if:

_____

_____

_____

_____

_____

Mother

What has been your greatest accomplishment?

_____

_____

_____

_____

_____

What is something you would like to accomplish in the future?

_____

_____

_____

_____

_____

_____

Daughter

What has been your greatest accomplishment so far?

_____

_____

_____

_____

What is something you'd like to accomplish in the future?

_____

_____

_____

_____

_____

_____

#1 daughter

 Mother

Who was your best friend when you were your daughter's age?

_____

_____

_____

What are the qualities you liked most about them?

_____

_____

_____

What is your favorite memory involving them?

_____

_____

_____

Daughter

Who is your best friend?

_____

_____

_____

What are the things you like best about them?

_____

_____

_____

What are your favorite things to do together?

_____

_____

_____

Mother

What did you want to be when you grew up?

_____

_____

_____

_____

_____

How is your life different from that now?

_____

_____

_____

_____

_____

Daughter

What do you want to be when you grow up?

_____

_____

_____

_____

_____

What are some things you can do to achieve this?

_____

_____

_____

_____

_____

_____

Mother

What are three things you wish for your daughter?

1
_____

_____

_____

2
_____

_____

_____

3
_____

_____

_____

Daughter

What are three things you wish for your mom?

1 _____

_____

_____

2 _____

_____

_____

3 _____

_____

_____

Mother

What is something your daughter doesn't know about you?

_____

_____

_____

_____

Daughter

What is something you don't think your mom knows about you?

_____

_____

_____

_____

Mother

What are some toys, books, or keepsakes you saved from your childhood?

_____

_____

_____

_____

_____

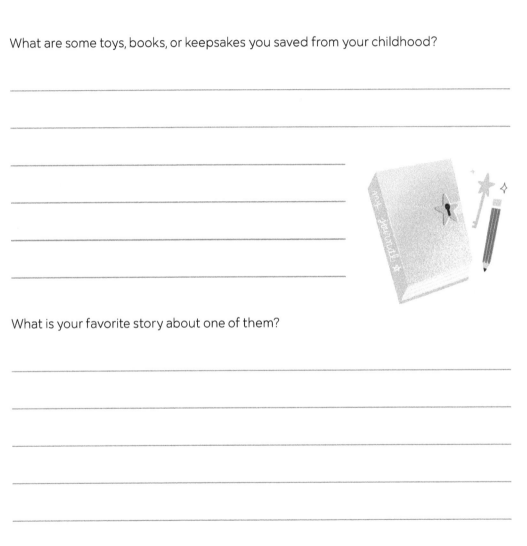

What is your favorite story about one of them?

_____

_____

_____

_____

_____

Daughter

What are some things that you want to keep forever?

_____

_____

_____

_____

_____

Why do you want to keep them?

_____

_____

_____

_____

_____

Mother

What is something that is hard for you to talk about?

_____

_____

_____

_____

_____

What would make it easier for you to open up?

_____

_____

_____

_____

_____

Daughter

What is something that's hard for you to talk about?

_____

_____

_____

_____

_____

What would make it easier for you to open up?

_____

_____

_____

_____

✧ **Mother** ✧

Draw your future self:

Daughter

Draw your future self:

Mother

What is a rainy day activity you'd like to do with your daughter?

_____

_____

_____

Make plans to do it together! Afterward, share your thoughts on how it went. What did you enjoy about it?

_____

_____

_____

_____

_____

_____

_____

 Daughter

What is a rainy day activity you'd like to do with your mother?

_____

_____

_____

Make plans to do it together! Afterward, share your thoughts on how it went. What did you enjoy about it?

_____

_____

_____

_____

_____

_____

 Mother

Were your parents strict when you were growing up?

_____

_____

_____

Did you have to do chores?

_____

_____

_____

Did you get an allowance?

_____

_____

_____

Daughter

When is your mom strict?

_____

_____

_____

Are you responsible for any chores? If so, which ones?

_____

_____

_____

Do you think kids should get an allowance? Why or why not?

_____

_____

_____

Mother

What is the best part of having siblings or cousins?

_____

_____

_____

_____

What are your favorite things to do with your siblings or cousins?

_____

_____

_____

_____

_____

Daughter

What is the best part of having siblings or cousins?

_____

_____

_____

_____

What are your favorite things to do with your siblings or cousins?

_____

_____

_____

_____

Mother

Describe what you think your life will be like in 20 years. Where will you be living? How will you spend your days?

_____

_____

_____

_____

_____

What will your daughter be like in 20 years?

_____

_____

_____

_____

Daughter

Describe what you think your life will be like in 20 years. Where will you be living? How will you spend your days?

_____

_____

_____

_____

_____

What will your mom be like in 20 years?

_____

_____

_____

_____

✦ Mother ✦

What are some things you can do to be a helpful member of society?

_____

_____

_____

_____

✦ Daughter ✦

What are some things you can do to be a helpful member of society?

_____

_____

_____

_____

 Mother

What is the best part of being a woman?

_____

_____

_____

_____

_____

What is the most challenging part of being a woman?

_____

_____

_____

_____

_____

Daughter

What's the best part of being a girl?

_____

_____

_____

_____

_____

What's the most challenging part of being a girl?

_____

_____

_____

_____

Mother

If you could travel back in time to one year in your life, which year would it be?

_____

_____

_____

_____

What would you do differently during that year?

_____

_____

_____

_____

_____

_____

_____

Daughter

If you could relive one day of your life over again, which day would it be?

_____

_____

_____

_____

What is something you would do differently on that day, and why?

_____

_____

_____

_____

_____

_____

Mother

What do you think your daughter's most prized possession is?

_____

_____

_____

_____

What is your most prized possession?

_____

_____

_____

_____

_____

_____

Daughter

What is your mom's most prized possession?

_____

_____

_____

_____

What is your most prized possession?

_____

_____

_____

_____

_____

_____

_____

 Mother

Who is your favorite singer/band?

_____

_____

What are some of your favorite songs?

_____

_____

_____

_____

What was the best concert you've ever been to?

_____

Who is an artist your daughter likes, but you don't?

_____

Daughter

Who is your favorite singer/band?

_____

_____

What are some of your favorite songs?

_____

_____

_____

If you could go to any concert, what would it be?

_____

Who is a singer you like, but your mom doesn't?

_____

Mother

What are some qualities you admire most in other people?

_____

_____

_____

_____

What qualities do you think people admire about you?

_____

_____

_____

_____

_____

 Daughter

What are some qualities you admire most in other people?

_____

_____

_____

_____

What qualities do you think people admire about you?

_____

_____

_____

_____

_____

Mother

What's the best thing about the country you live in?

_____

_____

_____

_____

_____

What is a law that you would change?

_____

_____

_____

_____

_____

Daughter

What is the best thing about the country you live in?

_____

_____

_____

_____

_____

What is a law that you would change?

_____

_____

_____

_____

_____

 Mother

What was the coolest technology you had when you were a child?

_____

_____

_____

_____

_____

What is your favorite technology today?

_____

_____

_____

_____

Daughter

What do you think is the coolest technology now?

_____

_____

_____

_____

What do you think technology will be like when you reach your mom's age?

_____

_____

_____

_____

Mother

What makes you sad?

_____

_____

_____

_____

What comforts you when you're sad?

_____

_____

_____

_____

 Daughter

What makes you sad?

_____

_____

_____

_____

What comforts you when you're sad?

_____

_____

_____

_____

_____

 Mother

Who is the funniest person you know?

_____

Who is the most generous person you know?

_____

Who is the most hardworking person you know?

_____

Who can you always count on?

_____

Who do you argue with the most?

_____

Daughter

Who is the funniest person you know?

_____

Who is the most generous person you know?

_____

Who is the most hardworking person you know?

_____

Who can you always count on?

_____

Who do you argue with the most?

_____

 Mother

What was your favorite sport or game to play as a child?

_____

_____

_____

What did you like about it?

_____

_____

_____

What is your favorite sport or game now?

_____

_____

_____

Daughter

What is your favorite sport or game?

_____

_____

_____

What are some reasons you like to play it?

_____

_____

_____

What is a sport or game you'd like to learn?

_____

_____

_____

Mother

How did your parents choose your name?

_____

_____

_____

_____

_____

If you could choose your own name, what would it be?

_____

_____

_____

_____

Daughter

Why did your parents choose your name?

_____

_____

_____

If you could choose a name for yourself, what would it be?

_____

_____

_____

If you have a child someday, what will you name them?

_____

_____

_____

 Mother

If you were stranded on a desert island, which three people would you want with you?

_____

_____

_____

How would these people make your experience on the island easier or better?

_____

_____

_____

_____

_____

_____

_____

Daughter

If you were stranded on a desert island, which three people would you want with you?

_____

_____

_____

How would these people make your experience on the island easier or better?

_____

_____

_____

_____

_____

_____

Mother

You have been invited to a fancy party. Design an outfit to wear:

Daughter

You have been invited to a fancy party. Design an outfit to wear:

 Mother

What about your childhood are you most grateful for?

_____

_____

_____

_____

_____

What is something you wish had been different?

_____

_____

_____

_____

_____

Daughter

What are three things you are grateful for?

1 _____

_____

2 _____

_____

3 _____

_____

What is something you wish was different about your life?

_____

_____

_____

_____

_____

_____

Mother

What is the most important thing you learned in school?

_____

_____

_____

_____

_____

What are some ways that education can be improved?

_____

_____

_____

_____

Daughter

What is the most important thing you've learned in school?

_____

_____

_____

_____

_____

What are some ways that you think your education could be improved?

_____

_____

_____

_____

_____

Mother

What would a fun mother-daughter bonding night look like? What activities would you do?

_____

_____

_____

_____

Make plans to do it together! Afterward, share your thoughts on how it went. What was your favorite part?

_____

_____

_____

_____

_____

_____

Daughter

What would a fun mother-daughter bonding night look like? What activities would you do?

_____

_____

_____

_____

Make plans to do it together! Afterward, share your thoughts on how it went. What was your favorite part?

_____

_____

_____

_____

_____

✧ Mother ✧

What are three places you'd like to travel to, and why?

1 _____

_____

_____

2 _____

_____

_____

3 _____

_____

_____

Daughter

What are three places you'd like to travel to, and why?

1

2

3

Mother

When were you most proud of your daughter?

_____

_____

_____

_____

_____

_____

_____

_____

_____

_____

_____

Daughter

When was your mom most proud of you?

_____

_____

_____

_____

_____

_____

_____

_____

_____

_____

Acknowledgments

This book is dedicated to my mother . . . for putting up with me during those angsty teen-age years, for being my lifelong cheerleader, and for setting an example of everything a good mom should be.

About the Author

 **Janene Dutt** is the creator of the popular humor and parenting site, I Might Be Funny, with more than half a million followers on social media.

She has zero self-control around a bag of Doritos, and she pours the milk before the cereal (don't judge). She thought a sloth was a mythical creature until two years ago, when her ten-year-old informed her that it is, in fact, a real animal.

She lives on a small island in the Pacific Northwest with her husband and three children. Her kids once asked her 159 questions in six hours and nearly made her lose her mind.

Visit her at IMightBeFunny.com.

CPSIA information can be obtained
at www.ICGtesting.com
Printed in the USA
LVHW010903130321
681243LV00004B/4